Also by Heidi Boerstler
Soaring! New Thinking on Leadership
Soaring! Act II: Leading into Leadership
Workbook for Transformational Leadership

We come with all these parts and no instructions how they go together.

Mark Nepo, American poet and philosopher

For Miriam, my inspiration for everything.

TABLE OF CONTENTS

PART FOUR: WAKE UP!

PART FIVE: YOU ARE WEAVING A UNIQUE TAPESTRY

PART SIX: BUILD GOOD TOOLS FOR OTHERS TO USE

ACKNOWLEDGEMENTS

Walking with a friend in the dark is better than walking alone in the light.

HELEN KELLER, TWENTIETH-CENTURY AMERICAN AUTHOR

For Scot, Cathy, Patrick, Jenean, and Margaret,

And for Mom, Dad, and Johnny

INTRODUCTION

No pessimist ever discovered the secret of the stars or sailed to an uncharted land or opened a new doorway to the human spirit.
HELEN KELLER, TWENTIETH-CENTURY AMERICAN AUTHOR

This book grew out of my work with leaders and future leaders in every kind of organization. They asked for a tool chest full of entrepreneurial practices and teachings to animate their leadership.

An entrepreneur is one who takes big risks. To animate is to revitalize, rejuvenate, and breathe new life into someone or something. This workbook focuses on entrepreneurship in leadership because this is what our rapidly changing environment demands. Entrepreneurs are needed to lead decision-making processes to do good for others. Therefore, it's necessary to go beyond a traditional leadership knowledge base.

Every leader is an artist with a tool chest of treasures and possibilities.

Each of us is unique, and uniquely gifted and talented, with an inventory of life experiences. From your inventory, you can discover gifts that can be of service to others. Wherever you are, you can animate your world. My intent in creating this workbook is to make you a master craftsperson, showing you a pathway and set of experiences that will illuminate and bring forth your hidden treasure and possibilities. All it takes to uncover your treasure is a clear eye, an open mind, and a willingness to risk searching in places other people are not able or willing to go.

You are here to make life better for having lived it.

You always have more to uncover.

HEIDI BOERSTLER

PART ONE
WHAT DO YOU RECOGNIZE?

Whatever you can do, or dream you can do, begin it. Boldness has genius, power, and magic in it.

JOHANN WOLFGANG VON GOETHE, NINETEENTH-CENTURY GERMAN WRITER

Practice One
Good Leaders Tool Their Crafts

Creativity is not a talent. It is a way of operating.
JOHN CLEESE, ENGLISH WRITER AND ACTOR

There is no single formula for good leadership. That is a good thing. Animating leaders use their unique tools creatively to do good for others. A tool is an instrument, implement or device, whether it's something imagined, such as a metaphor; an attribute, such as compassion, or something concrete, like a hammer. To *tool* means to practice, shape, fashion, or chase. Artistry is the creativity with which leaders tool their crafts. Every leader has materials for the work he or she is meant to do, the special tools within that weave the tapestry of his or her craft.

Artistry begins with experience.

What does it mean to tool your craft so that you can do good for others?_____

_____

_____

_____

_____

_____

_____

_____

Practice Two
What's In Your Tool Chest?

If you only have a hammer, you tend to see every problem as a nail.
ABRAHAM MASLOW, TWENTIETH-CENTURY AMERICAN PSYCHOLOGIST

A chest is a large, strong box used for storing or shipping. Tool chests are used for a trade or hobby or to store memories, dreams, and hopes for the future. A tool chest is always a treasure trove of mystery and possibility.

There are many types of tool chests, each type intended for a different use or purpose. One type is the portable toolbox, often called a hand box. The owner carries it from place to place and job to job. A portable toolbox has a handle on top and a hinge for security and safety.

Another portable tool chest is the tool belt or tool apron, worn by its owner and containing just what is needed for the moment or the job. Yet another portable tool chest is the bucket organizer, a canvas bag draped around a five-gallon bucket, its pockets filled with the particular tools needed for different job sites. Bucket organizers have open pockets in which the tools are always visible.

Large tool chests usually contain three or four tool drawers, and many also have cabinets for extra storage. They also have removable tote trays for parts and accessories. Tool chests can be made of wood, heavy metal, or lightweight plastic.

Every tool chest is different, unique to its owner's gifts and talents. It must be pruned periodically to remove tools that are outdated, in need of repair, or otherwise no longer usable.

Some tools are for a lifetime, intended to be available for the owner to use whenever needed. Other tools are for a season. Each tool has a special shape, size, and purpose. A tool that's useful in one context may be dangerous in another.

Many people in leadership positions are not aware of the entrepreneurial tools they have available or how they can be used to animate their world. Different tools till the soil, plow the ground, pour the water, feed new life, and illuminate with sunshine or other light.

Wise leaders choose well.

What does your tool chest look like? Is your tool chest a physical container, or is it metaphorical, or is it simply contained in your heart?_____

_____

_____

_____

What material is it made of? What tools are inside?_____

_____

_____

_____

Why does each tool belong there?_____

_____

_____

_____

Do you use a tool belt or apron in your daily work?_____

_____

_____

_____

What is your favorite tool? Your least favorite tool? What tool do you reach for first?_____

_____

_____

_____

Practice Three
Intent: Your First Tool For Animation

If I had eight hours to chop down a tree, I'd spend six sharpening my ax.
ABRAHAM LINCOLN, SIXTEENTH PRESIDENT OF THE UNITED STATES

What is your intent in this moment of possibilities?

Your intent is your first tool of mystery and possibility. You create a new future when you image it and then think forward from it. Possibility begins when you make the choice to risk opening your tool chest and reaching in for a tool, whether it's an attribution, such as compassion or courage; a metaphor for possibilities; or something concrete, such as a storyboard and colored pens.

In the real world, we lay down our paths as we go, not because we lack ability or skill, but because that's the nature of reality.

Nothing is fixed. Reality is how we choose it to be. It exists as infinite possibility. Our intent is the way we choose to give reality a form.

It's easier to change your mind than to change the world.

Step boldly into the intangible. Trust in it.

What tools inspire you each day?_____

_____

_____

_____

_____

_____

_____

_____

Practice Four
Good Tools Power New Beginnings

The expectations of life depend upon diligence; the mechanic who would perfect his work must first sharpen his tools.
CONFUCIUS, ANCIENT CHINESE PHILOSOPHER

Change is the nature of life. We watch the seasons change and the days turn to nights. Each moment is change, an opportunity for a new beginning. Leaders who animate see new ways to use their tools to do good for others, breathing new life wherever they are.

Leaders who animate choose their tools carefully.

When do you seek new tools?_____

_____

_____

_____

When do you use the same tool for every job? When do you decide a tool has outlived its usefulness?

_____

_____

_____

_____

What is your light source for darkness, such as difficult people or situations? _____

_____

_____

_____

What tools do you choose for the easy jobs? _____
_____
_____
_____

What are the different ways you can use the same tool?_____
_____
_____
_____

What tools do you carry with you daily?_____
_____
_____
_____

What tools do you continually have to polish and clean?_____
_____
_____
_____

What are your most important tools? Your least important ones?_____
_____
_____
_____

What tools must you force yourself to use?_____
_____
_____
_____

What tools do you choose for the big jobs? The small jobs? _____

_____

_____

_____

How do you sort your tools? How do you choose their spots in your tool chest? _____

_____

_____

_____

What are your tools for safekeeping? _____

_____

_____

_____

Which tools are always within easy reach? _____

_____

_____

_____

When is a tool dangerous? When is it full of possibilities? _____

_____

_____

_____

Which tools bring hope, expectancy, and fond memories? _____

_____

_____

_____

What are your power tools? Your action tools?_____

_____

_____

_____

Practice Five
Carry Rethinking In Your Tool Belt

In the beginner's mind, there are many possibilities. In the expert's mind, there are few.
ANONYMOUS ZEN MONK

Recognize that there is wisdom in changing your mind.

To repent means to rethink and to change your mind. Change means to become different. Most of us resist changing our minds. We fear it. Fearing change is human nature. We can see and realize choices. When we act from those choices, wisdom happens.

When do you choose to change your mind?_____

_____

_____

_____

_____

_____

_____

_____

Practice Six
Keep Clay In Your Tool Chest

Tools were made and born with hands. Every farmer understands.
WILLIAM BLAKE, NINETEENTH-CENTURY ENGLISH PAINTER AND POET

The science of neuroplasticity teaches us that our brains change in response to our experiences. It can happen at any age. Experience includes behavior, thoughts, emotions, and images. At any age, the brain can be trained to capitalize on possibility. In each moment, we can make the choice to move in a positive direction.

Our brain is an anticipation machine. We have approximately twenty thousand to forty thousand thoughts every day. What percentage is positive or useful? For most people, negative thoughts dominate. Constantly scanning for negativity comes at great cost. Negativity destroys creativity.

The brain changes in response to frequent practice. The more we perform a particular action, the more connections—called neural pathways—form. The stronger the link, the faster the message travels. Pathways can form at any age. Science has shown that our brains remain plastic and malleable throughout life. We have the power to create new habits and reap the benefits, whether we are twenty or eighty.

We can make the choice to change undesirable pathways into new and positive ones. Science teaches us that all systems are intended to move forward. We can change our experiences simply by changing our minds.

You have the power to reshape your brain.

What experiences will you choose today to move in a positive direction?_____

_____

_____

_____

_____

_____

_____

Practice Seven
Dig For Hidden Treasure

The river's now in me.
MARK NEPO, AMERICAN POET AND PHILOSOPHER

There is no one like you, nor has there ever been anyone exactly like you. You are unique, and part of you is old. The entire history of your genetic line is in your DNA. You have within you centuries of ancient memory, often called intuition. Each of us inherited a river of knowledge, a flow of patterns from many ages and sources: genetics (through our DNA), our evolutionary river; culture, the information passed along over hundreds of years; religion, the information revealed thousands of years ago; and family, the information passed along from decades ago.

We carry our past in our DNA. Our past lives in us as memories and old perpetuating emotions. None of us exists in isolation from our history. Our brains and bodies evolved and adapted to this river of information.

Each of us has an energy field of old that is still very much alive. All of this information flows to the unborn. Many people lead their lives as though theirs are individual life stories. But there isn't one single story. We are each part of a flowing river, with much history and many tributaries.

You are the latest expression of your ancestral line. Your ancestors are pushing you forward.

What are the special gifts and talents you received from your ancestors?_____

_____

_____

_____

What are your images of the ancestors who came before you?_____

_____

_____

_____

Practice Eight
Which Tools Build Bridges?

Handle your tools without mittens.
BENJAMIN FRANKLIN, ONE OF THE FOUNDING FATHERS OF THE UNITED STATES

What new beginnings are waiting for recognition?

Metaphysics is a branch of philosophy that studies the fundamental nature of being and the world. Metaphysics asks questions of human nature: What is ideal? What is the nature of being? What reality exists beyond the physical universe?

Metaphysics is a belief in the unity of the universe. Some have referred to tapping into that unity as "having a spacious mind." A spacious mind welcomes differences and builds bridges.

Building bridges requires tools for unity.

Which tools do you choose for building bridges?_____

_____

_____

_____

_____

_____

_____

_____

Practice Nine
Recognize Tools That Till Your Darkness

The problem is not to find the answer. It's to face the answer.
TERENCE MCKENNA, TWENTIETH-CENTURY AMERICAN PHILOSOPHER AND AUTHOR

Do good when you're in a valley.

New beginnings happen in darkness. Seeds are planted under the ground. Tilling the soil of self requires recognizing the darkness of your life, the struggles, failures, and disappointments that are a part of every life. Earning a degree and becoming a success are both good things to do but of themselves don't lead us to be our best selves. Failure is often our best teacher, if we let it be.

Facing darkness is always part of the journey. Facing darkness is where wisdom happens.

Everyone has experienced failure. Focus on a disappointment or failure that you've experienced. What tools helped you move forward again?_____

_____

_____

_____

_____

_____

_____

_____

Practice Ten
Carry Wading Boots For The Current

There are two ways to feel the wind: climb out into the open, and be still or keep moving.
MARK NEPO, AMERICAN POET AND PHILOSOPHER

Many people in leadership positions choose to stay with the safe and familiar rather than take risks. Are you one of them?

Some have identified two important life tasks. The first is to build an identity, including boundaries, safety, and success. The second is to find what that identity was meant to hold. This task asks what we're really doing when we're doing our first life task. It focuses on integrity, compassion, and honesty in our motives.

Many people in leadership positions never go beyond the first task, despite the fact that, at some point, they suspect their leadership is not fully working. That is why they stay on the same path, never leaving the bank of the river, never risking wading into the current. They continue to defend what they have invested so much to acquire.

I know many people like that.

Describe your wading boots. Are they made of willingness to risk, courage, patience, or something else? When do you put them on?_____

_____

_____

_____

_____

_____

_____

Practice Eleven
Have A Machete To Clear The Way

Courage does not always roar. Sometimes courage is the quiet voice at the end of the day saying, "I will try again tomorrow."
MARY ANN RADMACHER, AMERICAN WRITER AND ARTIST

A machete is a broad, heavy knife used as a tool for cutting through tough vegetation. An entrepreneur is one who takes big risks and clears the way for others. Taking risks is the foundation of growth. Entrepreneurial leaders guide others by going in front of or beside them through risk.

Many people choose to avoid risk, and they don't grow. Avoiding risk results in lost dreams.

It has been said that there are no second acts in life, but if you look around, you see that there are many second acts—and third acts and fourth acts. Read the biographies of successful people. Often the people who get what they're after are simply the ones who persevere; they stick around long enough. They just keep going.

It's a gift to be open to risking. A tiny seed of growth energy can grow a magnificent tree of possibilities.

Clear a new path.

Your greatest risk is not risking at all.

Describe your machete. Is it made of grit, steel, determination, or something else? When do you choose to use it?_____

_____

_____

_____

_____

_____

_____

_____

Practice Twelve
Always Carry A Magnifying Glass

A bad workman always blames his tools.
ENGLISH PROVERB

If you can't see what you're looking for, see what's there.
MARK NEPO, AMERICAN POET AND PHILOSOPHER

Awareness is our greatest tool for change.

Awareness is our knowledge or perception of a situation or fact. It's our realization, recognition, or consciousness. Awareness is not simply about the outside world. It's also an inner experience. Memories, fantasies, and plans dominate the lives of many people. Choosing to move from our memories of the past to anticipating the future also changes our awareness.

For animating leaders, choosing to be open to seeing other people and situations in new ways is so important. When our awareness changes, our experience changes as well. Changing the way we view the world changes the way the world feels to us.

We can choose to widen our lens to allow more light in.

Widening our lens is creativity.

Describe a time when you chose to see someone in a new way._____

_____

_____

_____

_____

_____

_____

_____

PART TWO
SEE THE POSSIBILITIES

A determined soul will do more with a rusty monkey wrench than a loafer will accomplish with all the tools in the machine shop.

Anonymous

Practice Thirteen
Have A Flashlight In Your Tool Belt

One only needs two tools in life: WD-40 to make things go, and duct tape to make them stop.
G. M. Weilacher, American philosopher

What life energies do you radiate?

Choose to be a light that shines in the darkness. You can't build something great on negative energy. Hurt and anger always show themselves eventually.

Like attracts like. Negativity attracts even more negativity. New beginnings are impossible in negativity.

Shining a light is always a good thing, no matter what is illuminated.

Describe your flashlight. What does it look like? How do you use it to build positive energy?

_____

_____

_____

_____

When do you use it? When don't you use it?_____

_____

_____

_____

_____

_____

_____

31

Practice Fourteen
Carry A Chisel: You Are What You Image

We need to count by touching, not by adding and subtracting.
MARK NEPO, AMERICAN POET AND PHILOSOPHER

A chisel is a long-bladed hand tool with a beveled cutting edge and a plain handle that is struck with a hammer or mallet in order to cut or shape wood, stone, metal, or other hard materials. Your image is a representation, portrayal, or depiction of you. What image of yourself have you chiseled? Is it fixed in stone? How would others describe you?

Examine the way your life choices reflect your image._____

_____

_____

_____

_____

Describe how you shape your image. Is it chiseled in stone?_____

_____

_____

_____

_____

Practice Fifteen
Your Body Illuminates You

Always carry a light bulb.
BOB DYLAN, AMERICAN SINGER AND SONGWRITER

Being aware of the fact that what your body illuminates about you is so important for leadership. Your carriage (the way you walk and stand) creates an image, so your body is a powerful leadership tool. Others notice and respond.

How do you stand when you're confident? When you're afraid?_____

_____

_____

_____

How do you walk when you're tense versus when you're relaxed? When you're happy versus when you're sad?_____

_____

_____

_____

How do you stand and walk when you're tired versus when you're full of energy? How do you stand and walk when you're angry?_____

_____

_____

_____

When you're lifting spirits, how does your posture change? Does your voice change? Do you hear others differently?_____

_____

_____

_____

Do you dialogue with your body? When do you ask your body for information? What thoughts and images are healthiest for you? Your body responds to your thoughts and aspirations._____

_____

_____

_____

What is your image of your body at this moment? What goals do you have for your body? How will achieving those goals impact your leadership?_____

_____

_____

_____

Practice Sixteen
Find Your Voice

The greatest defense is being who you are.
MARK NEPO, AMERICAN POET AND PHILOSOPHER

Be the original you are.

What does it mean to bring forth you, someone who is an original, who has never been and never will be again?

You always have time to animate those you lead and breathe new life into them.

You don't become good by trying to be good but by finding the goodness that's already within you and by allowing that goodness to emerge. The clearer we are about who we are, the more energy we have to use for good.

How you react to people and situations, especially when challenges arise, is the best indicator of how deeply you know yourself.

You find your voice by recognizing and using it.

What tools tell you who you are?_____

_____

_____

_____

_____

_____

_____

_____

Practice Seventeen
Scrape The Paint

You can have all the tools in the world, but if you don't genuinely believe in yourself, (they're) useless.
KEN JEONG, AMERICAN ACTOR, COMEDIAN, AND PHYSICIAN

How do you know who you are not?

Recognizing our unique gifts and choosing to use them to do good for others requires letting go of who we are not. Many people look outside themselves for approval. When we need outside approval to define ourselves, we lose our integrity, and we shift with the prevailing winds.

Sadly, it's not only possible to live a life other than one's own but most people do.

Scrape off the paint of who you are not.

When do you choose to scrape off the paint of who you are not?_____

_____

_____

_____

_____

_____

_____

_____

Practice Eighteen
Trust That You Have The Right Tools

The most persuasive tool you have in your arsenal is integrity.
Anonymous

A life spent making mistakes is not only more honorable but more useful than a life spent doing nothing.
George Bernard Shaw, twentieth-century Irish playwright

Choose life without knowing.

When you begin something new, you can't be sure how things will turn out. The only thing you can be sure of is that no matter how things turn out, they probably won't be exactly the way you imagined them.

When you begin something new, a little voice inside may tell you that you don't have the right tools for the job.

You have a choice. Choose life without knowing, learning from both joy and sadness. Or choose not to play at all.

When do you hold back, thinking you don't have the tools?_____

_____

_____

_____

_____

_____

_____

_____

Practice Nineteen
Carry A Stance Of Forgiveness In Your Bucket Organizer

A sword is never a killer. It is a tool in the killer's hands.
SENECA, ANCIENT ROMAN PHILOSOPHER

Bucket organizers carry tools for the big, hard jobs. Animating leaders choose a bucket organizer carrying a stance of forgiveness.

Has anyone ever betrayed you? Whatever happened in the past, good or bad, that was then, and this is now. Many people live in bondage to the past. They can never forget it, never get over it, and never get beyond it. They are locked into unforgiveness. Unforgiveness limits their choices and minimizes potential. When we cling to hurts, we don't move.

That's why choosing a stance of forgiveness matters. Forgiveness is not forgetting or excusing. Forgiveness is making the choice to let go. It's a shift in perspective that redirects your future.

A shift in perspective is a new beginning.

Describe a stance of forgiveness. Is it hard or soft—a stone or a rose or something else? Why is it meant for your bucket organizer?_____

_____

_____

_____

_____

_____

_____

_____

PART THREE

BEGIN WITH YOUR HEART

You are made for something good.

ANONYMOUS

Practice Twenty
Have Tools For Seeing Possibilities

That's what we all are. Amateurs. We don't live long enough to be anything else.
CHARLIE CHAPLIN, TWENTIETH CENTURY ENGLISH ACTOR AND COMEDIAN

Work for a spell with a man under harsh conditions, and you get to know his true nature.
MICHAEL McGARRITY, AMERICAN WRITER

What tools show you the way forward?

Possibility carries hope, potential, and likelihood. When you carry the tool of possibility, you mix in the yeast that gives rise to hope and belief in a new beginning. Possibility requires patience, restraint, and wisdom to wait for the rising.

What are your tools of possibility?_____

_____

_____

_____

How do you carry them?_____

_____

_____

_____

Are your tools of possibility with you all the time, or do you keep them for special occasions?_____

_____

_____

_____

Practice Twenty-One
How Do You Welcome Others?

Life is a succession of lessons (that) must be lived to be understood.
HELEN KELLER, TWENTIETH-CENTURY AMERICAN AUTHOR

Do you only learn from those who love you?

Your friends are your kindred spirits, your confidants, and your allies. Your enemies are those who challenge you. They are your antagonists, your adversaries, and your foes.

Welcome both your friends and your enemies. Good friends help you remember who you are. Your enemies challenge your ego and your sense of self-importance. They also offer opportunity for reconnection, reconciliation, and forgiveness.

Good leaders have welcoming tools for the hard moments.

Which of your tools do you use to welcome those who confront you and challenge you?_____

_____

_____

_____

_____

_____

_____

_____

_____

Practice Twenty-Two
Carry Tools That Soften Your Heart

We shape our tools, and afterward, our tools shape us.
MARSHALL McLUHAN, TWENTIETH-CENTURY CANADIAN PHILOSOPHER

How you know anything is how you know everything.

Master craftspeople know this wisdom. It's how you build something great. Building greatness requires softening our hearts.

What tools soften your heart? Our hearts hold the core tools of our compassion, our kindness, our tenderness, and our spirits. Sadly, much of the world is trapped in cynicism. Many of us have stopped listening to our hearts.

When you choose to use your tools to love someone or something every day, your energy will lift others.

What act of kindness will you choose today?_____

_____

_____

_____

_____

_____

_____

_____

Practice Twenty-Three
Keep Your Assumptions In Removable Trays

Sin has many tools, but lie is the handle (that) fits them all.
EDMUND BURKE, EIGHTEENTH-CENTURY IRISH STATESMAN AND PHILOSOPHER

Good leaders seek the truth.

Assumptions are ideas we accept as true without proof. Each of us has assumptions, so it's important to recognize them and evaluate them for truth. We make assumptions about such things as how best to live, the right thing to do in a specific situation, and so forth. Our assumptions form our life patterns.

Many people are unaware that they make assumptions.

What do we know about our assumptions? We know that they always limit us and that they are often wrong. We move in the direction of our assumptions, so it's important to recognize and examine them.

Our assumptions become manifest in our choices.

Keep your assumptions in removable trays.

How do you examine your assumptions for truth?_____

_____

_____

_____

_____

_____

_____

Practice Twenty-Four
What Tools Ignite Your Passions?

Do not wait; the time will never be "just right." Start where you stand, and work with whatever tools you may have at your command, and better tools will be found as you go along.
GEORGE HERBERT, SEVENTEENTH-CENTURY ENGLISH POET AND ANGLICAN PRIEST

The times you feel best about yourself are when you're on target with your passion, your spirit, and with what you just know. Your passion makes you feel alive. Passion is the inner fire that gives you a sense of freedom and accomplishment. Doing what you're passionate about transforms your life. It transforms how you view your past, your present, and your future.

Your passion ignites who you are.

What tools help you feel most alive?_____

_____

_____

_____

_____

_____

_____

_____

Practice Twenty-Five
Where Is Grace In Your Tool Chest?

Who is to say the effort to be real isn't the beginning of grace?
MARK NEPO, AMERICAN POET AND PHILOSOPHER

Grace means living in the moment. It means engaging reality as it really is without wishing it were other than it is. It's the state of mind of the ballerina totally absorbed in the dance or the wide receiver going up for the ball.

Sadly, most of us are worriers. We worry about what will happen tomorrow. We want security. We hoard. Worry is human nature.

Worry destroys the grace of living in the moment. Although we often worry, for most people there are times of the day or specific activities or locations in which we might have that experience of being in the moment.

Animating leaders understand that breathing new life requires living in the moment.

What are your tools for being in the moment?_____

_____

_____

_____

_____

_____

_____

_____

Practice Twenty-Six
Compassion And Humility Are Tools

All streams flow to the sea
Because it is lower than they are.
Humility gives it its power.
LAO-TZU, PHILOSOPHER AND POET OF ANCIENT CHINA

Animating leaders breathe new life into things wherever they are. Compassion and humility are tools for true leadership: the tenderness, mercy, warmth of compassion, and the meekness and humbleness of humility.

Compassion and humility are key tools for the master craftsperson. Both require intent and the wide lens of awareness to hone.

Describe someone you admire who chooses compassion and humility._____

_____

_____

_____

_____

_____

_____

_____

Practice Twenty-Seven
Name Your Tools For Courage

Success is not final, failure is not fatal; it is the courage to continue that counts.
WINSTON CHURCHILL, TWENTIETH-CENTURY BRITISH PRIME MINISTER

Courage is the foundation of new beginnings. It involves making the choice to go forward despite doubt and fear. Movement changes how we view our circumstances.

Moving forward broadens our angle of vision.

When you move forward, a new path will appear. If you stop too soon, you will never reach the summit.

Describe a time when you moved forward despite doubt and fear._____

_____

_____

_____

What tools helped you move forward?_____

_____

_____

_____

Practice Twenty-Eight
Anger Closes Your Heart

Keep away from angry, short-tempered men, lest you learn to be like them and endanger your soul.
PROVERBS 22:24

Anger is the first response you feel when you do not get your way; that was true when you were two years old and is true of you today. Anger is the greatest obstacle to forgiveness, kindness, compassion, humility, and wisdom. It keeps us from opening our hearts. Anger keeps our focus on narrowness rather than connection.

Anger is based on fear.

What is your image of yourself when you are angry?_____

_____

_____

_____

_____

_____

_____

_____

Practice Twenty-Nine
What Is Distracting You From Your Core Purpose?

Just trust yourself,
Then you will know how to live.
Johann Wolfgang von Goethe, nineteenth-century German writer

Be clear about what is important.

Are you exhausted at the end of the day? Do you seldom have a moment for yourself? You may be paying too much attention for too little.

Distraction from your core purpose is your greatest enemy.

What in your life no longer serves you well yet consumes an enormous amount of life force and energy?_____

_____

_____

_____

_____

_____

_____

_____

Practice Thirty
Carry Honesty In Your Hand Kit

Don't go around saying the world owes you a living. The world owes you nothing. It was here first.
MARK TWAIN, NINETEENTH-CENTURY AMERICAN WRITER AND HUMORIST

By becoming less, you become more.

None of us operates totally beyond self-interest. It's human nature; pretty much all our lives are filled with concern over ourselves. We just have to be honest about it. The problem comes when we say our only motivation is doing good for others. That's denial. Some of our motivations are always about our egos.

The next time someone criticizes you, blames you, or calls you names, instead of immediately defending yourself, do nothing. Doing nothing for a moment may feel uncomfortable (like diminishment). But then, if you stay with it, you may feel an inner strength. You have not been diminished at all. In fact, you have expanded. You come to an amazing realization. Nothing real has been diminished.

Remember, your work is what you do. It's not what you are.

When do you leave behind your honesty tools?_____

_____

_____

_____

_____

_____

_____

_____

Practice Thirty-One
Freedom Tools: Your Childhood Passions And Heroes

When was the last time you sang?
QUESTION PUT TO THE SICK BY A NATIVE AMERICAN MEDICINE MAN

What do our childhood passions and heroes have to do with our lives? Everything. The stories we tell about them shape us profoundly. We tell stories about our passions and heroes, except we don't tell them as stories but as facts and truths. They are stories that help shape our lives and determine the kinds of people we will be. We don't invent the stories of our childhoods by ourselves; we also learn them from others.

Childhood stories have enormous power. Do you tell sad stories of your childhood passions and heroes, or are your stories of freedom, good, and triumph?

How do we preserve values such as compassion, courage, kindness, and so forth? We tell stories about them, stories of heroes in our families, communities, and among our friends.

The stories you tell connect to who you are at the deepest level.

Those stories are in your tool chest. They help answer such questions as: Who am I? What am I here to do? And where am I going?

What stories do you tell about your childhood passions and heroes?_____

_____

_____

_____

_____

_____

_____

_____

PART FOUR

WAKE UP!

Most people never run far enough on their first wind to find out they've got a second.

WILLIAM JAMES, NINETEENTH-CENTURY AMERICAN PHILOSOPHER AND PSYCHOLOGIST

Practice Thirty-Two
Take A Hammer And Demolish Your Ruts

If you are going through hell, keep going.
WINSTON CHURCHILL, TWENTIETH-CENTURY BRITISH PRIME MINISTER

When does the seed of possibility decay, waste away, and die?

Why do some people with talent and opportunity go nowhere, while others with far less ability manage to overcome great obstacles and carve out good lives for themselves and others? The rut rule states that unless you do what you're capable of doing, you'll stay in a dark tunnel. A rut is a hell chosen by those people who have become comfortable with nothingness, with no challenges, with sameness, with narrow, predictable ways of life, unending routines, and unchanging attitudes. A rut is an unlived life.

Being in a rut is a choice. No one is there unless he or she chooses to be.

Better to risk something and fail than risk nothing and succeed at an unlived life.

Describe a time when you took a hammer to your rut._____

_____

_____

_____

_____

_____

_____

Practice Thirty-Three
Pride Can Destroy You, But It Is Always In Your Tool Chest

We don't let go and trust until we've exhausted our egos.
ANONYMOUS

Pride is defined as the quality of having an excessively high opinion of oneself or one's importance. Pride is arrogance, vanity, hubris, conceit, and being lost in comparisons. Each of us is pride. Each of us is also humility and meekness.

Probably the most courageous thing you'll ever do is accept that you're just yourself.

What is your image of yourself when you are full of yourself?_____

_____

_____

_____

What is your image of yourself in humility?_____

_____

_____

_____

Practice Thirty-Four
When Do You Cling?

I envy the tree, how it stretches but never holds.
Mark Nepo, American poet and philosopher

Clinging is in your tool chest, but it's a useless tool. Get rid of it.

It's human nature to cling and hold on, not wanting things to change. Of course this fails, and things do change.

We can't stop life from flowing. But we stay stuck, considering what was as a loss. Clinging and holding on only make this worse. New things come, but many of us focus only on what we don't have.

I know many people like that.

At any moment you can make the choice to animate your world. You have a choice in how you view your circumstances, how you treat others, and how you move forward.

When do you cling to what is safe and familiar?_____

_____

_____

_____

_____

_____

_____

_____

Practice Thirty-Five
What Frees You From The Need To Control?

We must take the current where it serves. Or lose our ventures.
WILLIAM SHAKESPEARE, SIXTEENTH-CENTURY ENGLISH POET AND PLAYWRIGHT

Trying to exert control limits your life.

When you do this, you set up resistance. Resistance drains your energy and limits you. Instead of trying to force solutions, begin by imaging possibilities you like, and then live as though they have already occurred.

Where in your life do you need control?_____

_____

_____

_____

_____

_____

_____

_____

Practice Thirty-Six
Choose Tools That Connect Systems

What lies behind us and what lies before us are tiny matters compared to what is within us.
OLIVER WENDELL HOLMES JR., TWENTIETH-CENTURY AMERICAN JURIST

We humans are emergent systems. *Emergent* means something that is waiting to happen. In emergent systems, everything is connected to everything else and happening together.

Animating leaders understand that breathing new life into things, or revitalizing them, means working with emergent systems. Work groups, relationships of every kind, and our brains are all emergent systems.

In emergent systems, people come together, and what is waiting to happen can become manifest and greater than the sum of their parts.

What tools do you use for connection?_____

_____

_____

_____

_____

_____

_____

_____

Practice Thirty-Seven
When Do You Stand Tall And Face Life Confidently?

Do not let what you can't do interfere with what you can do.
JOHN WOODEN, AMERICAN BASKETBALL COACH

Facing life is exhilarating. Facing life means mastering the anxiety of taking a risk. We are not happy when we run away. Facing life is saying, "This is what I want my life to be." Sadly, many people react; they do not act. They spend their lives reacting to circumstances and always consider themselves victims.

It's easy to find doubters who will reinforce our fears.

Facing life is animating. Watch a baby take his first steps. He is proud of himself, moving in the moment from a crawling person to a walking one.

What are your tools for confidence?_____

_____

_____

_____

_____

_____

_____

_____

Practice Thirty-Eight
When Do You Learn From Those Who Are Not Like You?

Only when I stop collecting evidence do the stones begin to speak.
MARK NEPO, AMERICAN POET AND PHILOSOPHER

Life is not perfect order. It's characterized more by exception than by order. People who do not follow rules are exceptions.

Good leaders recognize that finding truth is not always about seeing cause and effect and making things fit. It's more often about reconciling contradictions.

Most of us ignore the truth when it suits our interests.

Because nature exhibits more exception than order, we often learn best by recognizing and embracing the exceptions. Exceptions make us rethink our definition of *normal*. Our daily experience with the world involves a large amount of variation. And yet we have a long history of excluding those who don't think or behave as we do, such as the disabled or mentally challenged.

Observe how some people treat those who can do nothing for them. It's a true measure of their character. Most of us always treat well those we want to do something for us.

What assumptions do you make about people who are not like you?_____

_____

_____

_____

When do you make the choice to learn from those who are not like you? _____

_____

_____

_____

Practice Thirty-Nine
What Tools Mentor Others?

One of the greatest and simplest tools for learning more and growing is doing more.
WASHINGTON IRVING, NINETEENTH-CENTURY AMERICAN AUTHOR AND HISTORIAN

A master craftsman mentors his or her apprentices. It's how apprentices learn the standards of excellence for their trade.

But the true mentor does more than set standards for the trade. A true mentor has the courage to tell you that your age, fame, and professional status are not the important things. The real question is: who am I before I am any of those things? A true mentor has the humility, compassion, and wisdom to challenge you with the possibility that you are more and can be more than you currently are.

But you have to do the work. A mentor lets you know that you have the tools to face your darkness and be all right.

What are your tools for mentoring others?_____

_____

_____

_____

_____

_____

_____

Practice Forty
You Are Not That Important, And Your Name Is Written In Heaven

Every strike brings me closer to the next home run.
BABE RUTH, BASEBALL PLAYER

A paradox is a contradiction, a conflict.

Reality is paradoxical. Each of us is a paradox, a puzzle of generosity and greed, light and darkness. Do you really know what is good and what is bad as well as you think you do? If we are honest, everything is a contradiction. We are all a mixed blessing, a mixture at the same time of good and bad, blessing and curse.

Something seen one way can have a completely different meaning viewed another way. The question for leaders is how to embrace paradox and use it to do good for others

Describe areas of paradox in your life._____

_____

_____

_____

_____

_____

_____

Practice Forty-One
Have Tools For Your Fears

Fear is, I believe, a most effective tool in destroying the soul of an individual, and the soul of a people.
ANONYMOUS

For many people, fear is a constant companion. They don't know how not to worry, or how to motivate themselves without being afraid. They are living a false life, not living as who they really are. When you're living a false life, you're going to worry. There is a relationship between the fears many people have and the false lives they choose to live.

Fear changes the way you relate to others and to the world.

Many fearful people don't know they're afraid. They learned as children that the world is a frightening place. It's how they learned to live. No wonder many people don't risk, don't welcome possibilities. A stance of fear paradoxically closes you off to creativity. You're unavailable, closed, shut off.

Many people hunch over when they're afraid; they don't stand straight. They crouch in a self-protective stance.

Is it human nature to be in an open or in a crouched position? We learn to crouch very early in life.

_____

_____

_____

_____

What's your image of a crouched position? Even expecting new possibilities, you let go of some of the crouching and fear._____

_____

_____

_____

91

When does your mind take you into a self-protective mode?_____

_____

_____

_____

When are you aware of fear?_____

_____

_____

_____

How do you get to a safe place?_____

_____

_____

_____

Practice Forty-Two
Find Teachers Everywhere

You are the laboratory and every day is an experiment.
Go and find what is new and unexpected.
JOEL ELKES, AMERICAN ARTIST AND PHYSICIAN

You can learn from anything and anyone.

Be willing to experience.

Almost everything we want to do has been done before. Why do we fail to ask those who have done it? We often think we're unique in our experience. That is our ego. We are not unique. Because we believe our experience is unique, we fail to recognize the lessons others have to teach us. Recognize that there is no way to prepare for unexpected teachers and teachings except to keep your mind open and welcoming.

Where do you find your teachers?_____

_____

_____

_____

When are you willing to experience new teachers and teachings?_____

_____

_____

_____

Practice Forty-Three
Which Tools Connect You To Your Calling?

I have a thing for tools.
TIM ALLEN, AMERICAN ACTOR AND COMEDIAN

Animating leaders understand that work has two aspects: craft and calling. You need both. Craft includes knowledge of how to use the shovels, tillers, hoes, hammers, nails, saws, levelers, and so forth that you need for your craft. Calling asks whether what you're doing has meaning and purpose for you.

Facilitating finding a calling is rarely part of a leader's job description, but most often, lack of meaning and purpose demoralizes departments, people, and organizations.

What tools do you use to find a calling in your work?_____

_____

_____

_____

_____

_____

Practice Forty-Four
Tool Your Craft To Inspire Others

Integrity is the ability to listen to a place inside oneself that doesn't change, even though the life that carries it may change.
RABBI JONATHAN OMER-MAN, AMERICAN WRITER AND SPIRITUAL COUNSELOR

Are you someone others aspire to be?

When you're in a leadership position, it's a great mistake to want to be like everyone else. That is not your job. Your job is to set standards that those below you have to stretch to meet.

Great craftsmen do this when times are hard. They uphold values they may find old-fashioned. They may represent virtues they don't even possess. They are mature. When no one chooses to be a leader, standards get lowered. Those who look up to you aren't taught what they need to know.

Master craftsmen tool their artistry with depth, wisdom, and character.

Looking back over your life, what are your memories about good leadership? What picture immediately flashes? How did the leader you remember walk, stand, and speak to you?_____

_____

_____

_____

_____

How did he or she show confidence in you? Belief in your ability? Kindness? Compassion?_____

_____

_____

_____

_____

PART FIVE

YOU ARE WEAVING A UNIQUE TAPESTRY

If you would create something, you must be something.

Johann Wolfgang von Goethe, nineteenth-century German writer

Practice Forty-Five
How Do You Use Papier-Mache?

I tried so hard to please that I never realized no one is watching.
MARK NEPO, AMERICAN POET AND PHILOSOPHER

How do you choose the masks you wear?

We all wear masks, like papier-mâché, tight on our faces. Most of us are controlled by them. Our masks determine much of what we say or don't say, do or don't do. Our masks of papier-mâché, paint, and clay are all the many faces we appear to be. Most people's life work is protecting this self-image. A mask is not bad; it's just not true.

We wear masks because we are afraid. They're manufactured and sustained in our minds. We always have tools we use to put them on. But our masks can and will die, as all fictions eventually die.

We mistake our masks for reality, but who we are always comes out in the end.

The question is: am I free to be anything other than the masks I wear? Others notice and respond to the masks you wear.

What is the mask you wear in your work? How did you learn to put it on?_____

_____

_____

_____

What image or picture is associated with each mask you wear?_____

_____

_____

_____

What mask do you put on every day? What does your daily mask do for you?_____

_____

_____

_____

What are the assumptions you make in wearing a particular mask?_____

_____

_____

_____

What would happen if you left it at home?_____

_____

_____

_____

Practice Forty-Six
What Tools Quiet Your Mind?

Please remember that it is what you are that heals, not what you know.
CARL JUNG, TWENTIETH-CENTURY SWISS PSYCHIATRIST AND PSYCHOLOGIST

What is your image of a quiet mind? What picture comes to you?

A quiet mind can best connect to who you are at the deepest level.

Do you choose to quiet your mind? What tools do you choose? Remember that we humans are a band of brothers. We all breathe the same way. With every breath, we can choose to move in a new direction. Your breath is the core of your body language. It reflects your state of being.

Your breathing is only as good as your posture.

Experiment with this exercise: Begin by closing your eyes and noticing your breath. Watch your breath as it goes in and out. Image a sponge wiping your brain clean again as you breathe.

Describe your mind when it's quiet. _____

_____

_____

_____

_____

_____

_____

Practice Forty-Seven
Nature Speaks To Who You Are

Nature chose for a tool, not the earthquake or lightning to render and split asunder, not the stormy torrent or eroding rain, but the tender snow-flowers noiselessly falling through unnumbered centuries.
JOHN MUIR, NINETEENTH-CENTURY AMERICAN NATURALIST

Nature speaks to the hope deep within us. Have you ever lost yourself while gazing at a sunset or lying on your back in fresh grass? Nature brings us back to our senses, if we let it.

Hope is a tool for new beginnings. Nature gives us tools for how to be still, how to be graceful in the moment, and how to be who we are.

When do you use nature's tools for being?_____

_____

_____

_____

_____

_____

_____

Practice Forty-Eight
Polish Your Listening Tools

Repetition is not failure. Ask the waves, ask the leaves, and ask the wind.
MARK NEPO, AMERICAN POET AND PHILOSOPHER

Listening means paying attention in order to hear. It's so important for good leadership. But we are often not aware of what good listening means. It's the choice and the privilege of wisdom to listen. Active listening requires energy. It's a skill you can learn and an art that requires practice, an awareness of judgment. Leaders need both.

Wise people can be silent even when they are speaking. They have a willingness to create space to hear you. This realization can bring you greater awareness of how you respect and esteem yourself and others. As a leader, the way you attend to the one who is speaking presents a clear picture of your integrity. Others notice and respond.

Listening is a skill that can be learned:_____

_____

_____

_____

Do you listen to the words you speak and the manner in which you speak them? Others may hear your words in ways you did not intend them._____

_____

_____

_____

How do others know you're not listening? What is your image of not listening? We know when others are not listening to us._____

_____

_____

_____

How do others know that you're listening to them? How do they know you're paying attention in order to hear? Is it your intent to hear people all the way through? Many people plan what they're going to say before the other person is finished speaking._____

_____

_____

_____

Listening is an art:_____

_____

_____

_____

When are you aware of judgment?_____

_____

_____

_____

Practice Forty-Nine
Every Word Counts

One does not become enlightened by imagining figures of light, but by making the darkness conscious.
CARL JUNG, TWENTIETH CENTURY SWISS PSYCHIATRIST AND PSYCHOLOGIST

Your words tell a story. Research has demonstrated that when people are shown an object or a face or given a food, their assessment of how much they like it, how valuable they see it, and so forth is affected by what they are told about it. People want to know where things came from, how they were made, who made them, and what people did with the choices they had. The stories you tell about these things impact how people feel and what they understand about your work and about you.

How others feel and what they understand about you and your work with others for good affects how they value it. Humans want to connect. It's human nature. Personal stories make the complex more tangible, create synergy, and offer insight into things that might otherwise go misunderstood.

Your work with others does not exist in a vacuum. You tell a story about yourself and your work with every conversation, e-mail, photo, and video.

They are all bits and pieces of the tapestry you weave.

How do you use your words as tools to do good for others? _____

_____

_____

_____

_____

_____

_____

_____

Practice Fifty
Unlearn

Opportunities are usually disguised as hard work. So most people don't use them.
ANONYMOUS

To unlearn is to repent, to rethink, to reexamine, or to change your perception. Unlearning is a choice. It's also a key tool for becoming a master of animating leadership.

We unlearn when we discard information previously learned, such as bad or dated information, or information that is no longer true.

Unlearning is a tool for both the recognition and illumination of truth.

Many people choose to cling to beliefs they know are no longer true. They don't make the choice to unlearn.

Embracing truth is a tool for transformation.

Describe a time or situation in which you made the choice to unlearn something you previously believed to be true._____

_____

_____

_____

_____

_____

_____

Practice Fifty-One
When Do You Unplug Your Screens?

Any tool is a weapon if you hold it right.
ANONYMOUS

Most of us live in a world where we're always connected to screens of various kinds. Life has become more crowded. The more time we choose to spend in the online world, the less time we have for our own thoughts and our own inner world. Animating leaders understand the danger. We can't breathe new life into anything when we rely on screens and sites to tell us who we are and what we think.

We are losing our uniqueness and our unique gifts and talents.

Many people in leadership positions are never away from their screens.

Describe the power of your screens. When do you rely on your screens? When do you rely on your own investigation?_____

_____

_____

_____

When do you disconnect from your screens? What happens when you do?_____

_____

_____

_____

Practice Fifty-Two
When Do You Need New Tools?

To do good work, one must first have good tools.
ANONYMOUS

What new beginnings are you choosing now? What tools do you have available to you? Do you need new tools, or do you simply need to clean, polish, and shine what you already have?

_____

_____

_____

_____

What tools and people support your work for good? How does each plant a seed in you every day?

_____

_____

_____

_____

How are you currently manifesting your leadership? Do you have the tools you need for animation?

_____

_____

_____

_____

If you need new tools, where will you find them? How will you know they are effective?

_____

_____

_____

_____

Practice Fifty-Three
Name Your Tools For Hope And Expectation

The greatest discovery of my generation is that a human being can alter his life by altering his attitude.
WILLIAM JAMES, TWENTIETH-CENTURY AMERICAN PHILOSOPHER AND PSYCHOLOGIST

How do you stay in a new reality when the old reality is still happening? Change requires time, repetition, and consistency.

With every step, you radiate an image. With every word you speak, you radiate an image. You can radiate beauty or ugliness.

When we expect to find good things, we usually do. When we expect to be miserable, we usually are.

Understanding this concept is foundational for good leadership. Animating leaders expect good things, good people, and good outcomes.

Name three things that were good for you today. Why were they good?_____

_____

_____

_____

Name three things you're grateful for today. Why are you grateful?_____

_____

_____

_____

Practice Fifty-Four
Do Your Tools Enslave You?

No amount of thinking can stop thinking.
MARK NEPO, AMERICAN POET AND PHILOSOPHER

We are all addicted to something: work, a good self-image, exercise, worry, memories, procrastination, alcohol, and so forth. Our addictions are our own worst enemies. They are personal tools that enslave us, erode our free will, and destroy our spirits.

The same tool that is effective in one context can enslave us in another.

Addictions compel us to give energy to things we don't truly desire. And yet, paradoxically, addictions can lead us to compassion, humility, and new beginnings.

When do your tools enslave you?_____

_____

_____

_____

_____

_____

_____

PART SIX

BUILD GOOD TOOLS FOR OTHERS TO USE

We shall not fail or falter; we shall not weaken or tire…Give us the tools and we will finish the job.

Winston Churchill, twentieth-century British Prime Minister

Practice Fifty-Five
Choose Tools That Make People Better At Something They Want To Be Better At

There is great satisfaction in building good tools for other people to use.
FREEMAN DYSON, AMERICAN THEORETICAL PHYSICIST AND MATHEMATICIAN

Which of your tools inspire others to believe in themselves?

A myth, in the context of leadership, is what I believe and what we believe about ourselves in the organization, whether or not what we believe is true. This is important because what I believe about myself (or my group or organization) will influence my attitudes, my behavior, and my future. What can you share that would help others? What tools do you have for them? What kind of knowledge can you share?

Breathing new life into something happens when you learn something and then turn around and teach it to others.

Teaching others does not subtract value from your leadership. It adds to it. When you teach someone how to do your work, you generate faith in them…and confidence in his or her own work for good.

When you do this, you become a mythmaker.

Best of all, when you share with others, you learn in return.

Doing well and doing good are absolutely compatible.

What tools do you use to help people begin to believe in themselves?_____

_____

_____

_____

_____

_____

Practice Fifty-Six
"Yes!" Is Your Risking Tool

You miss 100 percent of the shots you never take.
WAYNE GRETSKY, HOCKEY PLAYER

For most people, *no* comes easier than *yes*. When you begin with yes, you're accepting risk, new experience, and a willingness to move. You can't begin seeing or understanding anything if you begin with *no*. *Yes* is acceptance, which means you have not presumptively labeled something as good or bad. *Yes* is leaving the field open.

Yes is freedom; *no* is constriction.

Yes is expansion and grace in the moment.

Yes is your heart.

Describe a time when you said, "Yes!" _____

_____

_____

_____

_____

_____

_____

_____

Practice Fifty-Seven
Big Dreams Are Big Tools For Passion

If not now, when?
ANONYMOUS

If you don't have a big dream, you just exist. You have lost your passion.

Describe a big dream._____

_____

_____

_____

What stops you from achieving it?_____

_____

_____

_____

Practice Fifty-Eight
You Always Have More To Uncover

Let the beauty of what you love be what you do.
RUMI, THIRTEENTH-CENTURY PERSIAN POET

Animating leaders are found in all walks of life—in every occupation, at every age, with every disability, and at every organizational level. Do you know any animating leaders? They are the master craftspeople breathing new life into their work and having fun at what they're doing.

Work is play for these master craftspeople. They teach their crafts to others by example. In my experience, all people who have found their way to animating leadership have also had many failures. The difference is that they didn't give up; they viewed failure as a necessary part of obtaining wisdom.

Choosing to breathe new life into things wherever you are is living your best self.

You always have more to uncover.

Describe someone you know who is living his or her best self._____

_____

_____

_____

_____

_____

_____

Practice Fifty-Nine
Name Your Tools For Moving

The flower doesn't dream of the bee.
It blossoms and the bee comes.
MARK NEPO, AMERICAN POET AND PHILOSOPHER

Recognize which tools are for moving forward and which tools are for staying put. Make sure you know the difference.

Move! It's the basic rule for creating something new. When you begin moving, things begin to happen. It's called synergy. Synergy shows us that when we begin with a small motion to sweep or rake or dig, there is a ripple effect. Simply by picking up the rake, connections begin. Slight adjustments synergize a system. Synergy recognizes even small movement as new opportunity, as possibility.

What are your tools for moving?_____

_____

_____

_____

_____

_____

_____

_____

Practice Sixty
Have Good Tools For Wandering

I am as all mortals are, unable to be patient.
PABLO NERUDA, TWENTIETH-CENTURY CHILEAN POET

To wander means to roam, drift, prowl, choose to get sidetracked, and to be open to surprise. To become good at anything—anything—you have to wander, to take on a beginner's mind. You have to embrace being a novice, someone who is just starting to learn. At a certain point, you just have to give up control and let it happen, or it won't. You have to choose to surrender. Trying something new makes you confront your fears. Saying yes is empowering. You create new energy, the energy of new beginnings.

It does not get any better than that.

What are your tools for wandering? _____

_____

_____

_____

_____

_____

_____

_____

Practice Sixty-One
You Are Here To Make Life Better For Having Lived It

The instant fish accept the fact that they will never have arms, they grow fins.
MARK NEPO, AMERICAN POET AND PHILOSOPHER

Animating your world means recognizing that at any moment you can make the choice to open your heart, stretch out your hands, and broaden your mind. The question for leaders is: first, what tools facilitate that recognition, and, second, what tools facilitate movement?

Here is the lesson: live your life. The more you do, the more you accomplish, the more productive you are, and the more you give to others, the less energy and time you will have to stew over the past and fantasize about what might have been and how others have hurt you.

You're here to play the game of life with ever-increasing skill. That is playing the game. Playing the game means knowing there's a reason you're here. And it means not having the illusion that you're in charge. Playing the game is cleaning your pipes of sludge to expose your light and your wisdom. Playing the game is leading yourself and others, tilling the soil of yourself in order to plant seeds of new beginnings. You don't get to pick the time you play. You only get to play.

Your challenge is to live the best you can, recognizing that your life is bigger than you are. Playing the game is your goal.

What are your most important tools for playing the game of life? _____

_____

_____

_____

_____

_____

_____

_____

135

Practice Sixty-Two
What Are You Leaving Behind You?

What is in your heart and what people receive from you is what makes you.
PATRICK MILES, FRIEND

Clarify your own wisdom. Ask yourself these questions: Does knowing you leave kindness, compassion, and goodness in the lives of others? Or does knowing you bring pain and suffering to others' lives? How many lives have you touched?

What are you leaving behind you in the lives of others?_____

_____

_____

_____

Who have you lifted up?_____

_____

_____

_____

Who have you not lifted up when you had the opportunity?_____

_____

_____

_____

How many lives have you touched?_____

_____

_____

_____

Honesty is the net by which we fish the deep.
MARK NEPO, AMERICAN POET AND PHILOSOPHER

ABOUT THE AUTHOR

Heidi Boerstler, DrPH, JD, is professor of transformational leadership and health law and ethics at the Business School, University of Colorado Denver. Her degrees are from Northwestern University (BA), Johns Hopkins University (BS), University of Denver (JD), and Yale University (MPH, DrPH). Boerstler is also a consultant to health-care, business, and legal organizations. She lives in Denver, Colorado.

BIBLIOGRAPHY

1. Boerstler, Heidi. Soaring! Act II: Leading into Leadership. Denver, CO.: CreateSpace Books, Anne Miriam Boerstler Foundation, 2012.

2. Boerstler, Heidi. Soaring! New Thinking on Leadership. Denver, CO.: CreateSpace Books, Anne Miriam Boerstler Foundation, 2011.

3. Boerstler, Heidi. Workbook for Transformational Leadership. Denver, CO.: CreateSpace Books, Anne Miriam Boerstler Foundation, 2013.

3. Braden, Gregg. Isaiah Effect. New York: Three Rivers Press, 2000.

4. Brooks, David. The Social Animal. New York: Random House Trade Paperbacks, 2011, 2012.

5. Chicago Manual of Style, 14th edition. London: University of Chicago Press. 1993.

6. Collins, Dianne. Do You Quantum Think? New York: SelectBooks Inc. 2011.

7. Gilbert, Daniel. Stumbling on Happiness. New York: First Vintage Books Edition, 2009.

8. Gopnik, Alison. The Philosophical baby. New York: Picador, 2009.

9. Leher, Jonah. How We Decide. Boston, New York: Mariner Books, 2009.

10. May, Gerald. Addiction and Grace. New York: Harper One, 1988.

11. May, Gerald. Will and Spirit: A Contemplative Psychology. New York: Harper One, 1982.

12. Nepo, Mark. The Book of Awakening. San Francisco: Conari Press, 2011.

13. Rohr, Richard. Falling Upward. San Francisco: Jossey-Bass, 2011.

14. Rohr, Richard. The Naked Now: Learning to See as the Mystics See. New York: Crossroads Publishing, 2009.

15. Shapiro, Rabbi Rami. Forgiveness. Traverse City, Michigan: Spirituality Health Books, 2011.

16. Shapiro, Rabbi Rami. The Sacred Art of Lovingkindness. Woodstock, Vermont: Skylight Paths Publishing, 2006.

17. Siebert, Al. The Resiliency Advantage. San Francisco: Berreu-Kooehler Publishers, Inc., 2005.

ADDITIONAL NOTES

Made in the USA
San Bernardino, CA
20 October 2018